DAVID JOHNSON

ACER

NOV. 11, 1949

SEPT. 3, 1990

PRAISE FOR *A Quilt for David*

"A stunning homage to people with AIDS, *A Quilt for David* is a wrenching investigation into the experience of 'the innocent victim': white straight women and closeted white men who had to retain an inhumane level of capitulation to patriarchy in order to be eligible for compassion. By unearthing the Kimberly Bergalis case from its tomb of ash, Reigns reminds us how easy the path of false accusation remains, in this case at the expense of gay men with AIDS subjected to diabolical cruelties and exploitation. He reveals again how hypocrisy coheres communities by relying on cliches of femininity, bias, and repressive loyalties."

—Sarah Schulman, author of *Let the Record Show: A Political History of ACT UP New York, 1987-1993*

"One of the most important roles a poet can assume is that of emotional historian. Reigns certainly understands that notion in this necessary and genre-bending book which powerfully blends poetry, non-fiction, and reportage to reexamine the maligned story of David Acer and arrive at a truer truth with compelling honesty and the utmost compassion for all."

—Richard Blanco, 2013 Presidential Inaugural Poet, author of *How to Love a Country*

"This writing is energetic, alive, and uncensored. Reigns has studied poetry and deeply researched a moment in history. *A Quilt for David* breaks traditional structure and cracks open what we thought we knew of the past. Through poetry and prose we glean a deep understanding of a life misunderstood and mischaracterized. Reigns goes to the mat to find out what really happened, and with his expert pacing we're right there with him."

—Natalie Goldberg, author of *Writing Down the Bones: Freeing the Writer Within*

"Reigns lifts David Acer thirty years after his death to show the naked cost of violent, unexamined public opinion around the catastrophe of AIDS. This poetry masterfully documents the tangle of hatred and lies haunting a generation of survivors. I am often grateful for what poems give to me, most especially the ones in this book."

—CAConrad, author of *AMANDA PARADISE: Resurrect Extinct Vibration*

"Told in short, occasionally haiku-like entries, Reigns has done what literature should: put the reader into the mind, the suffering, of another human being. Stripped down to its essentials, this retelling of one man's terrible suffering is also a portrait of those who used him as a scapegoat because, given the times, they could."

—Andrew Holleran, author of *Chronicle of a Plague, Revisited: AIDS and Its Aftermath*

"Like so many of us born into the age of AIDS, who saw the epidemic from childhood and grew up in a world forever changed by loss, Reigns is searching for the stories of our ancestors. This work is a glorious attempt to regain one of those stories; to ask what we do in the name of fear, and who is deemed worthy of our compassion. A brave and harrowing recalculation of humanity in an inhuman time."

—Justin Elizabeth Sayre, author of *From Gay to Z: A Queer Compendium*

"Much too long, suffering has been part of our collective queer legacy. We weather the storm of insult to character and seemingly irreconcilable injustice in tandem with the hope that the arc of time will bend towards justice; our time is now. *A Quilt for David* is a posthumous journal of vindication."

—Brontez Purnell, author of *100 Boyfriends*

A Quilt for David

A Quilt for David

STEVEN REIGNS

CITY LIGHTS BOOKS | San Francisco

Front cover photograph of David Acer from *Odontos*, 1974, Ohio State University College of Dentistry Yearbook, courtesy of The Ohio State University Libraries Archives.

Frontispiece image is a rubbing of David Acer's grave marker in Sarasota, Florida, and is part of Steven Reigns's *The Gay Rub*, an exhibition of rubbings from LGBTQIA+ landmarks around the world.

Cover design by Gerilyn Attebery

ISBN: 978-0-87286-881-6
eISBN: 978-0-87286-856-4

Library of Congress Cataloging-in-Publication Data

Names: Reigns, Steven, author. | Scholder, Amy, editor.
Title: A quilt for David / by Steven Reigns ; Amy Scholder, editor.
Description: San Francisco : City Lights Books, 2021. | Includes bibliographical references.
Identifiers: LCCN 2021012917 | ISBN 9780872868816 (paperback)
Subjects: LCSH: Acer, David, 1949-1990—Poetry. | LCGFT: Poetry.
Classification: LCC PS3618.E557 Q55 2021 | DDC 811/.6—dc23
LC record available at https://lccn.loc.gov/2021012917

City Lights Books are published at the City Lights Bookstore
261 Columbus Avenue, San Francisco, CA 94133
www.citylights.com

DEDICATED TO

My parents, Barb & Chuck,
who instilled values that helped me
look beyond a headline

and

Tom & Wayne,
who believed in me and told tales of how gay men
got silenced and sidelined

In 1990 a young HIV-positive woman in Florida claimed she was a virgin and that her infection came from her gay, dying dentist. The media believed her, seven others came forward, and a monster was born.

PREFACE

FROM 2000 TO 2013 I provided HIV testing, education, and counseling to people living in Florida and California. I personally tested over 9,000 people. One day, an anxious young woman came in after a dental procedure, fearful that she could have contracted HIV. I gave her my standard educational talk, using colloquial language, explaining that HIV is transmitted through five fluids: cum, pre-cum, vaginal fluid, blood, and breast milk. I told her how HIV needed a window into the body like a cut or sore. It turned out that her results were negative, which didn't surprise me.

But her fear reminded me of a story I saw when I was in the eighth grade. A young woman appeared on *A Current Affair* and *Inside Edition*. She said she was a virgin and that she got HIV from her dentist. Another woman, much older, made the same accusation.

I was certified by health departments in Florida and California; I gave presentations at national conferences and was trained by some of the best educators in the country. I couldn't imagine how HIV would be transmitted from a dentist to a patient. Even if the dentist didn't wear gloves, passing on the virus seemed virtually impossible. HIV is a very weak virus outside of the body and dies quickly. Being exposed to HIV doesn't always mean infection. So

I wondered, how did those two women get it? Did a psychopathic dentist purposefully infect his patients? I thought of the dentist in *Little Shop of Horrors*, victimizing his patients, blood splattering everywhere.

I also wondered if those two women told the truth. I can't count how many clients I counseled who got infected while cheating on their spouses, infected them, and then feigned ignorance about what happened. I comforted many of those spouses, bound to secrecy by HIPAA confidentiality. There was also a young man, just eighteen years old, who infected his pregnant girlfriend. His own transmission came from a rape at a detention center, which he disclosed only to me, fearing ridicule if he told anyone else. There are lots of reasons to hold onto a secret; sometimes, in keeping that secret, someone gets blamed for something they didn't do, and a history gets written.

In 2008, I started searching for the name of the dentist, Dr. David Johnson Acer, and the women who accused him of giving them HIV: Kimberly Ann Bergalis, who claimed to be a virgin, and a grandmother, Barbara Webb. I was amazed to find such a trove of tributes, articles, artwork, photos, a play, and references to books dedicated to Kimberly Bergalis. There were statues of her, a beach bearing her name, and a cover story in *People* magazine. Very little was written about David Acer, the dentist.

Our knowledge of HIV transmission has progressed over the course of the epidemic, yet the story of the dentist victimizing his patients with AIDS in 1990 seemed immutable.

I found only one photo of David. I couldn't find quotes from him or his family. Who were these people, and what really happened? I wanted to find out, and I wanted to tell that story.

I flew to Florida, where I went through courthouse documents and researched at public and university libraries. I wanted to talk with David's family, friends, coworkers, and patients. In 2012, I ran an ad in a local paper with that one photo of David and said I was interested in talking with people who knew him. My phone rang often. Many called never having met him but wanted to give me their opinions or ask me why I was curious about a murderer. I received kinder calls from patients who reported benign memories of him being quiet and generous, giving discounts on dental work, or giving away extra theater tickets. I talked with employees who worked for him and I asked about the cleanliness of the office, the dentist's disposition, and his patients. I met with neighbors, good friends, and acquaintances, and eventually I found a man who had sex with David.

The only words I encountered that came directly from David were in a public letter written from his hospice bed, days before his death:

> *It is with great sorrow and some surprise that I read that I am accused of transmitting the HIV virus. . . . I am a gentle man, and I would have never intentionally exposed anyone to this disease. I have cared for people all my life, and to infect anyone with this disease would be contrary to everything I have stood for.*

David sounded kind, and his office didn't sound like a little shop of horrors. But the story about him was horrific.

A high-powered lawyer, who represented college student Kimberly, was clearly aware of the potential for settlement money in the part of Florida known as the Treasure Coast. There was a $3 million malpractice insurance to be considered, and whatever could be extracted from the health insurance company that referred clients to David's now-closed practice. Eventually, checks were written for $999,999 to Kimberly, Barbara, and another accuser, Richard. These checks were followed by an undisclosed sum of money, rumored to be $1.5 million, from the insurance company. But the crusades of the Rolls-Royce-driving lawyer and "I did nothing wrong" Kimberly persisted. They wanted to mandate that every HIV positive health-care worker disclose their status to patients. Even though, aside from their allegations, there were no other reported cases of dental transmission of HIV.

The stigmatizing amendment, offered by Senator Jesse Helms, mandated $10,000 fines and a ten-year minimum prison sentence for health-care workers who failed to disclose their HIV status. Kimberly, weighing seventy pounds, traveled eighteen hours on an Amtrak train, three months after having a priest give her last rites, and spoke on the Congressional House floor. Her testimony was twenty seconds and fifty-seven words. The decision could jeopardize the livelihood of HIV positive health-care workers, some of them accidentally infected while doing their jobs. The mandate did not go through. Years after Kimberly's death, her parents only go to a dentist with a posted sign saying he's HIV negative, and they get tested before visits.

While articles, essays, and books have been dedicated to the theory that David Acer is a killer, the facts don't bear that out. The more I discovered about this story, the more it appeared that Kimberly, Barbara, and the six others who blamed David for their infection could have been like so many of my patients who didn't disclose their own full stories of HIV infection. Each one of them—Richard Driskill, an unidentified man, Michael Buckley, Sherry Johnson, Lisa Shoemaker, and John Yecs Jr.—had their own circumstances and motivations to blame outside risk factors, to blame David Acer. Those facts, details, and data were overlooked, and an unquestioned narrative became historical record.

I decided to tell David's story as a way to counter the treachery of his end of life. Poetry wasn't just my beloved form of writing; it felt the best way to assemble the sparse information that existed without adding speculative details. The discrediting facts about the dental infection story were overridden by public emotions elicited by Kimberly's narrative. Poetry and poetic language compel our emotions. What if, through poetry, I could offer an equally empathic and compassionate view of David? These poems also serve as a way to memorialize him and what his story tells us about humanity, homophobia, and our history.

David Acer and Kimberly Bergalis died over thirty years ago. Some of the terribleness of that time may have been forgotten or unknown to readers of this book today. AZT was an AIDS drug that was fast-tracked for FDA approval, only to be determined more detrimental than helpful. Kaposi's Sarcoma or KS are disfiguring sores commonly associated with HIV infection and were therefore stigmatizing for those afflicted.

For all the people involved, and all the stories that were told, I've found that there were some well-meaning journalists and also sloppy researchers, unscrupulous lawyers, invasive private detectives, and people out for money. There was hatred of gay people, repressive parents, people wanting a perfect victim, mob mentality, and collective anxiety about HIV and what it meant about you if you contracted it.

What happened in that dental office and in that small town in Florida was happening everywhere. Who gets believed? Whose story do we prioritize over others? What risks do we forgive, and what risks do we punish? These are urgent questions relevant to our current pandemic as well.

Every detail in this book is based on fact. I decided not to use poetic license, to avoid adding fiction to a story already loaded with misinformation. In the course of my research, David became real to me. In some poems I address him directly. I tried to shred previous ideas, remove the stuffing, and rip out ill-aligned seams. I hope these patchwork poems give you an idea of that time and another way to remember David Acer.

—Steven Reigns, March 2021

A Quilt for David

Silence, driving home after your diagnoses, engulfed the car moving up the coast. Your green, four-door Accord humming up the interstate. Periodic fits of crying, road out of focus from tears. No cell phone to call someone and confide. Even if there had been, you would have kept the news a secret. The doctor-to-driveway commute gave time to think about this death sentence. No one recovered from the disease. No pills, cure, or even hope. Walked into your front door, greeted by Ginger, your cocker spaniel's panting and wagging. Slumped onto the foyer floor, petted her, cried, confided in Ginger through the night.

162 in your graduating class
161 men
159 white people
1 Black person
1 Asian person

Part of the accelerated class of 1974
received doctorate diplomas
in March, not June.
Common for Ohio State graduates
you joined the army.
Captain in Germany for two years.

Not the time or place to be out.
Experimentation and affairs hidden.
The youngest in your class,
you were described as agreeable, shy.
Your white lab coats always pressed and exceedingly neat.

You worked hard to finish school, build a practice, and create a family of coworkers. Kimberly returned home, told her mother the dentist seemed like a nice guy. That mother, under oath, would later say you were "a pretty amicable guy." The personnel were "great . . . it was kind of like a family type thing." All these years later, they still honor you. Saw how every word was twisted, every quote was suspect. So your staff stopped talking. Silence more loving than defense.

His lips never moved from hers, never wandered down her neck to nipple. Hands never traveled under her pants and panties. In the two years of their dating, he had only kissed her. Didn't want more. In 1987, Kimberly entered the college infirmary crying. Told a mental health worker she asked that boyfriend if he had a disease or was gay. He broke up with her. Sent her crying to seek counseling. Four years later, when she needed answers about a man, the dentist, she didn't ask. She accused.

I'd sew a quilt for you.
I would grab a needle,
put the thread in my mouth,
moistening the fibers together.
I'd pierce into the eye.
I'd hem, backstitch, sidestitch
a remembrance of you.
I'd put your name in large letters
wanting no one to forget you died of it
too. I'd sew you into that larger quilt because
no one else has. I'd select patterns, design a quilt
representing your lifelong loves.
Kimberly has four panels, photos, and a large starfish.

I'd sew for you, thimble on my thumb,
push the threaded needle through the fabric.
If I were to prick my finger
and bleed, I wouldn't regret
a single drop of blood or effort.

At the dental society's annual Christmas party, you stood alone, watched the ice cubes melt in your plastic cup. How were you to socialize when the men in the room talked of women, raising kids? There were your boating and golf games, but there was also your gayness that could be revealed and reviled. Others would later suspiciously say how you "just stood there," wanting to be a part of the crowd and not knowing how.

You bought the nicest house on Alamanda Way. Furnished it with modern American furniture, sheer curtains, a full-size pool table, played Yes's *Owner of a Lonely Heart* on the stereo, and fenced the backyard. Got a pilot's license, ski boat and truck to pull it, and a tennis club membership. If you weren't going to have a partner, weren't going to have a family, you were going to create one. Bought a cocker spaniel, named her Ginger for her color.

Dark muddy brown urine, fever not breaking, every joint in your young body in pain. You sought help from the doctor on base. You had Hepatitis B. It could have been from food; it probably came from a man. You must have changed *him* to a *her* or feigned ignorance all together. As the Q-tip slid into your urethra and later as blood filled a vial, you regretted the encounter, hated your gayness, your secrets, and wished you were different.

Investigators questioned Kimberly's father, asked whether he had touched her. George Bergalis protested he was being victimized twice. First, the news about Kimberly. Second, their accusations. He said her sickness would have been easier to accept if she'd been a slut or a drug user. Maybe one night she met a man. He talked of his travels, bought her drinks, escorted her home. Kissing led to an invitation to come inside. How could she explain that to such a father? He called David a murderer. Believed anyone HIV-positive who practices medicine was an executioner.

What if Kimberly's mom heard the rumors that her daughter liked Mexican men—Latin, Latinos, migrant farmworkers? These were not the kind of men Kim was encouraged to date. Rumored at her high school to have been slutty—maybe Anna Bergalis heard that too. What could have been happening in Kim's room down the hall, or in her dorm room at the university known as a party school? When Kim testified, put her hand on a Bible she believed in, perhaps it was easier for her mom to hear about the dentist.

In 1989, George Bergalis attempted to make a dental appointment and was declined. He was told the dentist was in the hospital. To ensure a safe sale of the business, patients were told David had cancer. George directed the Fort Pierce Finance Department and said to his staff, "You watch. The guy's probably got AIDS."

Greg Bergalis said, "No one
should have their
daughter's life taken away."

Everything dies too soon, is
taken away too soon,
every daughter
is taken away.

Harriet Acer's son
studied German in high school,
completed dental school and military,
piloted her in a plane.

Everything dies too soon, is
taken away too soon,
every son
is taken away.

Brownish-purple lesions covered your legs and throat. Your hair patchy, deep circles under eyes, weight loss hollowed your checks, front teeth protruded. You lost a career, future, and your looks. You avoided mirrors. During long days spent in hospital beds, nothing distracted you except the RCA television. When male orderlies checked your vitals, you'd cower, thinking how you must look to them. Before the loss of weight and hair, before Kaposi, before AIDS, you might have turned their heads, been courted, been seen as superior or at least an equal.

Educated to heal, to provide comfort,
to treat injuries of the mouth.
There was one you couldn't handle.
The sole KS sore on the roof of your mouth.
Soon there were four.

On an evening in May
you carted a dental electrocautery home.
An electric device
that cauterizes wounds.
In the dimly lit bathroom mirror
you used it to singe your palate.
Red hot electrical heat on wet tissue.
Repeated the procedure, burning
each lesion.
Dentist, heal thyself.

Indelible ink on skin declares passionate love, loss, heartbreak, devotion to one's mother, military service, a penchant for self-decoration. At their worst, tattoos numbered Jews, gypsies, and gays. In the holocaust of AIDS, William F. Buckley Jr. suggested tattooing the infected. To serve as a warning, like cautionary tape, road flairs, or traffic cones. March 18, 1986. I wonder if David read the *New York Times* that day. Set down his morning cup of coffee, pulled up the right sleeve of his robe and looked at his bare forearm. Wondering what might one day appear on his freckled skin.

Mary Malloon, an immigrant.
David Acer, gay.
Not popular traits for their times.
Her body housed bacteria,
his body a virus.

Typhoid Mary died nine years
to the day David was born
in Ohio, November 11, 1949.

She, a young cook,
didn't stop
when she was told
of the poison running in her.

David asked his doctor,
who didn't know his real name,
if he could continue.

Maybe David, like Mary, infected
those he served. Maybe
instruments weren't cleaned well enough,
maybe the numb fingertips of neuropathy
were pierced or cut accidently.
Maybe it did happen,
not to all, but maybe a few.
The others rode it for the money
they might not
live to enjoy.

Before her diagnoses Kimberly was training to be an actuary, studied the consequences of risk. Barry Manilow played while she studied in Gainesville, not knowing the risks. Six hours south, you were taking in bathhouses and bedrooms. You, unknowingly, took the same risks young men and women took across the county. The same risks Kimberly would later be accused of. All of them emboldened by youth and a mute president. If she knew the risks maybe she would, as an actuarian, have gone to you anyway. One hundred seventy-one infected dentists practicing on thousands of patients with zero transmissions.

The next morning blood spotted her underwear. It wasn't her time of the month; it was from the night before. He had rubbed up against her, petting her. The CDC report of the incident stated she did "not think his penis penetrated her vagina but is not sure."

The hope and promise of a drug, AZT, the only one available, prescribed six days before your thirty-eighth birthday. The social worker noted your situation: lonely and isolated. By then KS covered your body. The meds caused headaches, nausea. You endured it all to prolong the life you built—thriving practice, tennis, pilot's license. Was there a party, streamers, confetti, and cake? Who celebrated your birthday with you, six days after the drug that was poison, assailed your bloodstream?

Ulcers from worry and lies
lined your stomach. A toxic
taxing of accumulated stress;
your closeted life and love of men,
treatments given under pseudonyms.
Alcohol, the social lubricant of the shy,
didn't help the healing of your stomach.
Friends talk about you in Fort Lauderdale,
drink in hand, dancing with smaller, Latino men.
Those men a reprieve from repressive Stuart, Florida, and
a distraction from Jodi, the charismatic blond
who lived with you for six months, a
house husband but ultimately too much
of a party boy. Worry over your hidden life,
health, the failed relationships, and what had become of you.

Typhoid Mary didn't believe
when they told her to
stop preparing food, to
stop practicing her only
line of work. She knew
nothing of
transmission.
David didn't stop either.
Told of necessary precautions.
Took them.
The difference:
Mary infected people
unknowingly. David
might not have
infected anyone
at all.

One plus three for area code plus seven digits.
What must it have been like
for David to dial those
eleven numbers, the spinning of
the rotary for each one, as he lay in the
VA hospital bed, four hours away
from work, home, and dog.
While the phone rang, did he think
about hanging up, backing up,
keeping it all a secret, and suffering alone?
His mother Harriet
answered, and he told her he
was gay, has AIDS, was dying.
She had visited two months
before, and he had said nothing.
Holding the receiver, the
spiral cord twisting and tangling below,
he said his plan had been to say
nothing, he hoped a
cure would come and that
his life would go back
to normal.

On August 27, admitted to the hospital in Juniper, David was finally out; mother, stepfather, and siblings knew. Past coworkers knew he was dying, some knew he was gay, many speculated AIDS. Towards the end of his life, the shackles of secrecy lifted. Health Department, attorneys, reporters shattered this secrecy with questions, subpoenas, cameras. His parents transferred him to the Hospice of Palm Beach County, his final residence, where secrecy was needed again, and he was admitted under a pseudonym. The same one he used at the start of his illness, a name he used out of fear of discovery. His moment of openness vanished.

Kimberly had a great memory,
didn't need to write down orders.
She could handle a party of six,
remembering each appetizer, entrée,
and any substitutes. The Pelican
Yacht Club wasn't her career but a
job she had for the summer.
A busboy worked there, thought
to have AIDS. We don't know
how Kimberly treated him. Did she avoid him
out of fear, overtip out of sympathy, or
flirt with the ultimate bad boy?
Busboy, bad boy? Maybe he was no boy at all.
Did coworkers talk with him, or did they
shun him out of fear, ignorance?
Maybe the yacht club was where Kimberly learned
how the infected were treated.

Your parents, Victor and Harriet, booked
a hotel near the hospital,
wanted to stay close to you,
where investigators
could no longer knock unannounced.
They feared it your last days.
Sixty pounds lost.
PCP pneumonia treatment again.
You were confined to bed,
a urinary catheter to piss.

Weeks earlier the Public Health Department
wanted you to go public,
wanted you to tell the world of your private illness,
that you were the dentist of the allegations.

You declined, your mother brought meals,
KS sores throughout your mouth.
White, thick candidiasis
coated your throat and digestive tract.
Lying in that hospital bed knowing
death was imminent,
knowing a wake, not of mourners
but revilers might follow.
You feared death,
the public,
and more pain.

A hospital staffer referred to you
in a chart as "this unfortunate gentleman."

Harriet Acer divorced, remarried, remained faithful to God, moved to be with her sick son. After she moved, he said it wasn't cancer as he had told her, it was AIDS. The family rallied, and David's older brother mailed his mother a book, *How Will I Tell My Mother? A True Story of One Man's Battle with Homosexuality and AIDS.* Trying to make sense of the situation, trying to understand, trying to be supportive, Harriet read every one of Jerry Arterburn's words.

You were born the year Polaroids
were introduced.
After your death
only a few photos of you are public. One
from college, another from a wedding
with boutonniere. Slowly dying in hospice—
nothing was instant—you were handed
a pad of paper to pen a note
to clients, the community,
to be published in the newspaper.
Pen moved across the page;
four days later you would die.

Between the pen ink and death certificate,
with the stark word AIDS,
your calm, round face
was shown on every TV news station.
Name and practice in every newspaper.
Your parents dealt with sickness,
the loss of their son,
and then the slaughter
of your life in public.

George Bergalis and his wife believed you were gay,
and when their daughter got sick
they pointed the finger at you, not Kim.
Your family was not on the news,
no photos of them, like the Bergalises
in *People* magazine, photos of
them caring for their
dying child. Kimberly

on the cover. Talk developed
of your drives to Lauderdale
where you'd cavort, court, and dance
with other men. Cameras
weren't allowed in bars,
no one wanting evidence
that could be used
against them.

The CDC gave six digits
to each of the infected
to track without using names.
Kimberly 242284, David 158093
One more digit and it could have been
a phone number.
But it wasn't a phone number,
it was a code, keeping
confidentiality while exposing
the most intimate of details.
David sat with Dr. Carol Ciesielski,
CDC medical epidemiologist,
and shared answers freely:
the precautions he took,
his diagnoses,
his parents moving in,
his sexuality,
and let them draw vials
of his infected blood.

Actually, David wasn't sitting
with Ciesielski.
He was in bed, dying.
The virus killing Kimberly
was killing him too.
In a CDC report
next to his number is a note,
the dentist reported
Kimberly's extractions
were a simple procedure,

no impaction,
just a pull of the pliers.

158093 didn't recall
any times he had injured
himself while practicing
or putting anyone at risk.
Under that number is
another dentist's note
about Acer's files,
"impressed with the
level of documentation."

Kimberly testified to
Congress, “I did
nothing wrong . . .
My life has been taken away.”

Then in a videoed deposition:
Q: Has anybody ever performed oral sex on you?
A: Yes.
Q: Was there more than one episode?
A: Yes.

She didn’t do anything wrong.
She did with that man, with other men,
what lovers do, she explored the
pleasures of the body. The clit has more nerve
endings than a fingertip.

She did what David had done, what
Barbara, John, Sherry, Lisa, and Richard
had done. They were alive and bright
and loveable and sexy, and they
shared of themselves, of their bodies what
the Lord, the gym, or genetics had given them,
with someone else or many others.

Nothing they
had done was wrong,
and the life
they knew
was taken
from them.

Painter Grant Wood saw the Dribble House when touring Eldon, Iowa. Sketched it on the back of an envelope, studied it the next day in oil on poster board. The figures he inserted were modeled after his sister, and his dentist, a man with pinched lips and bespeckled eyes. Wood spent hours in Dr. Byron McKeeby's chair due to his daily half cup of sugar in coffee. He even sprinkled sugar on his salads. Wood, a closeted gay man, studied that face leaning over him while his mouth gaped open. *American Gothic* changed McKeeby's life: he was forever recognized. Upset with Wood, they barely spoke for ten years. Sometimes a patient can change the trajectory of a dentist's life.

Bob Montgomery fought for her.
Took the case,
wrote documents, led proceedings,
did interviews, talked with the press,
handed out his card, smoked cigars.
He fought for her as if
she were his own,
but she wasn't. He had
his own son, infected as well.

Kimberly drove to Miami in her new car,
money provided by Montgomery.
She accepted the $5,000 as a gift
(or possibly a bribe).

"I don't know why; I just believed her."
Gut or guilt (or greed) made the
southern man believe.

Scott Montgomery died in 1992,
a year after Kimberly.
Did his father make tributes to him
in the newspaper? Sit by his bedside?
Was he treated the same way as she?
Was his illness deserved?
When Kimberly met Barbara,
she was relieved, said
"Thank God, there's

someone else to carry
the torch. I'm too tired."
As Kim was dying,
Barbara called her.
"I have a firm grip
on the torch."
What was she carrying?
What did that torch illuminate?

Barbara Webb's eyetooth broke during the pulling. David struggled to remove the upper tip. She described him having a "cold sweat." She asked if it was hard. He, using a hooked instrument, told her, "It's just a matter of leverage." Robert Montgomery represented Barbara Webb and Kimberly, and Richard, and then Sherry. Gave Kimberly money the same day he told her about results from the insurance's medical exam. She had venereal warts. Montgomery asked not only for an insurance settlement but also for mandatory testing. Using, as leverage, homophobia and Kimberly in a wheelchair on the congressional floor.

Bob Webb fills out crosswords
with his cocktail nearby.
Met his beloved on a blind date,
took her to a church supper. He, for the
second time in his life, baked
a pineapple-upside-down cake.

The second date ended with
playing chess in a bar. They
married in 1949.

He was an elevator engineer, retired
early, moved himself and the wife to Florida.

In August 1990, the *Stuart News* urged
Dr. Acer's patients to be tested.
He thought a test was silly.
"We're far too old to get AIDS."

His wife urged him, and on
Thursday, September 13, 1990,
they found out their results.

His wife received a call that the vial
holding her blood had been broken.
She needed to come back for another
draw. He escorted her.
After the blood had been drawn,
they were escorted to an office.
A doctor told them

there was no broken vial.
Everything felt upside down.

The husband and wife.
One retired, one working out
of restlessness, were brought
into the room together.
The nurse said, "I have good
news and bad news."
She might as well said,
"I have bad news and bad news."
Because Bob's negative status didn't
feel like good news.

When the doctor told
her the news, Barbara felt punched.
The doctor showed her the two
western blot results. Bob reached
over and held her hand.

Barbara "felt like one
of Dali's watches."
Two years later, he fills
out his crossword puzzles,
two million in their bank account from
the lawsuit, their sex life
ended due to fear.
"I can make a clock,
but I can't find a way
to turn back time."

Lisa Shoemaker, patient E, was the one the media least believed, yet she was the most forthcoming. Talked of the ex, her past, her jobs. She offered her truth, not a mythology. Montgomery didn't represent her. When insurance funds were doled out, she received very little. Two decades later she rescues stray cats, nurtures them back to health. When asked, she goes to schools, talks to students about HIV and the importance of safe sex. She advocates for adolescents with AIDS, lives with her boyfriend in Michigan, has grandchildren, and a pill regime. She periodically switches medication to avoid side effects, a viral load, an early death.

Michael Buckley could sell the moon even though he wasn't the owner. His journal notes him in a station wagon with another man. His girlfriend, Lisa Shoemaker, read it after her money went missing. He smashed her head into the wall. A gay club-goer was outraged to see Michael in a striped shirt on television blaming the dentist because he was "one of the biggest tramps in Port St. Lucie."

It has been long advised
not to beat a dead horse.
Senator Jesse Helms
ignored the idiom.
Stated David and people like him
should be horsewhipped.
Said this long after
David was dead.

The office where you
methodically took time with patients,
seeing only eight a day,
briefly became a nightclub.

Club Envy had an
all-ages night. Kids
younger than the age Kimberly
was when she was in your
chair, moved on the dance floor.
Young girls undid top blouse buttons
as soon as their parents dropped them off,
rolled up their shorts on the dance floor,
sweated under blacklights and mirror balls,
kissed with straight white teeth,
pressed their bodies together.

They know nothing about history.
They barely know the music
the DJ spins. They'll leave the club,
round the corner in the humid
Florida night, smoke cigarettes in the
lot where your patients parked.
Maybe they'll drink from a flask
that's been hidden in a young man's
cargo shorts pocket. Take gulps outside
the window patients once looked out from.

They know nothing of you or
how hated gays were back then
or what AIDS meant at the time. They

can't possibly imagine what it was like
for a man trying to make a living
with a deadly virus, for eight others
with a deadly virus looking
for someone to blame.

The young kids come every week for
the music, the lights,
the energy, flirtation, and
the bodies moving next to them on the dance floor.

Kimberly must have felt something
similar at college, dancing to late '80s music with her
girlfriends, flirting with men,
smoking pot, tasting cocaine,
maybe unbuttoning one
more button on her blouse.
Barbara said she was the original hippie.
Did she love to dance too?
John was a partyer.
Richard might have enjoyed a tune at the jukebox.
Lisa likes her Harley and heavy metal.
You went to discos in Germany
and Fort Lauderdale.
How drinking eased your awkwardness
enough to dance and hit on men.

All of you as innocent
as the revelers at Club Envy.
No one could have possibly known
when they danced in their youth

what was to come, how what they felt
couldn't be bottled or kept or captured.
That a virus would harm them all.

The chairs your
patients sat in were sold by
Dolphin Dental Supply
and purchased by other dentists.
Maybe one was sold
to a tattoo shop—
it could still be used, twenty
years later, when positive men
self-appoint bio-hazard tattoos.

After the nightclub closed,
your office became
a pool hall and arcade.

Two years, ten months, and twenty-nine days
from diagnosis to death,
David kept practicing.
Retired at forty to die.

From diagnosis to death,
was scared of small-town rumors and small-town mentality.
Retired at forty to die.
He used an alias at doctor's offices hours away from his home.

Was scared of small-town rumors and small-town mentality.
David said hiding his diagnosis was "lonely and isolating."
He used an alias at doctor's offices hours away from his home.
Kimberly, secretly sexually active, points her finger at David.

David said hiding his diagnosis was "lonely and isolating."
She pointed her finger at him.
From diagnosis to death was
two years, ten months, and twenty-nine days.

After her mother brushed her hair,
her father carried her body,
half its normal weight,
a skeletal sixty-five pounds, to bed.
Her father tucked her in,
"See you tomorrow."
Kimberly replied through blistered lips,
"Hopefully not."

Before the cocktail, when the virus kept multiplying like gremlins in the body. Before full, unfounded faith was put into AZT, Kim and Barbara were inundated with offers. Lemonade, aloe, barley, yams. Super-heating blood treatment. People wrote, called, and dropped by unannounced. As gay men died alone in hospices, hospitals, and homes across the country, people wanted to save these two women.

John Yecs was given the seventh letter of the alphabet, G. The CDC tracked and traced his medical records from rehab facilities to county hospitals. He sued the dentist, the rehab center who referred him. And all the while rumors and whispers abounded about his needle use and the long list of sex workers he'd been with.

Sherry Johnson, diagnosed after the media frenzy, said, "Thank God he's dead." Uttered God's name during the nightmare. Did Kimberly curse Him after her diagnosis? Did David pray during his months of secrecy? If sex was the act that infected them, each one separately, did they ever call out His name in gratitude? Thankful for that moment, lost in the pleasure of their bodies.

The interim dentist,
fresh out of college,
would later tell the media
she suggested better ways to clean instruments.
HIV lives only a minute outside the body.
She complained of dust on your instruments.
You complied, stopped using
alcohol wipes, purchased an autoclave.

A patient said you
weren't talkative but nice.
You would go out of your way to save her
office copies of *People* magazine.
Eight months after your death,
the weekly magazine's headline
was about you.

Kimberly is embodied in bronze and poised atop a rock, notebook in hand, socks folded, with slip-on Keds. A commissioned likeness from her eyelashes to bangs to French braid mounted outside her private grammar school. In her high school, rumors spread that she slept around. Below the statue, a plaque: *One life can make a difference.*

On the floor of Congress, she said, "I did not do anything wrong." Was he the one who did wrong? Facing death and mounting medical bills, was David supposed to forfeit his practice, his only income? Instead he took more precautions. Wore gloves and autoclaved more. A disclosure such as his would have been career death. David said he had ten positive patients, probably the only ones who would have then filled his appointment book. HIV was the new leprosy in 1989. In July 1999, Kimberly cheered when the Senate passed the bill, introduced by Jesse Helms, mandating ten-year prison terms and $10,000 fines for HIV-positive health-care workers who don't tell their patients.

To a group of school children Kimberly said,
"Everybody makes mistakes."

Harold Jaffe, CDC investigator, could have been a mercenary. As he finished his studies, a new disease consumed his career and the bodies of millions. Fresh with hope, full of promise, he was handed a case of a young girl with pretty brown eyes, who maybe under different circumstances he would have approached at a party, asked out for coffee. When the report came back that the woman, as pure as Mary, might not have been, did he solace himself with information that HPV might have been common for those infected by the virus? HPV doesn't come from nowhere. It, like the virus he was paid to track, has a source, has a reason. Gynecological exams showed a hymen broken from intercourse. A polite man, maybe it was too hard for him to out her; the thin, frail, young, dying woman with a crocheted blanket keeping her skeletal body warm, even in the Florida heat. Did he sacrifice one reputation for the purity of another? What did silence equal, and what did it matter who took what to the grave?

The court talked of DNA matching, how your virus matched that of Kimberly and Barbara and John and Sherry. The technology was new. DNA matching isn't as easy as matching socks. The first control group was national, comparing yours and Kimberly's HIV to those across the United States. They then compared those in Fort Lauderdale, West Palm Beach. A match. Dr. Lionel Resnick, a physician from Miami Beach, doubted the control groups. Thought residents of Stuart, Florida, could have a common strain. Drawing blood from support groups and gay bars, he found five individuals with virtually identical strains and no connection to you.

In the frenzy of a dying virgin and dying grandmother, the courts divided up responsibility. The lawyers divided up the money. Cases were closed, checks were written. Later, scientists stated that the CDC "did not perform enough control comparison to be sure that the virus . . . was not otherwise found in south Florida."

A casual cocktail conversation
can be twisted, made into good headlines,
and, with Edward Parson as a friend,
that is what happened.

Ed Parsons said he was a confidant of yours:
going out on your boat,
drinking and bar buddies.
In 1993, he told *20/20* about a
deathbed confession, that you talked
of Bergalis and Webb—the virgin and the grandmother.
Parson created drama on a bigger scale,
amplifying his tall tale to thousands.
You never knew the
name of your young accuser. You also died
long before Barbara Webb ever got tested.

Barbara Webb, the Mensa member, said you were the most boring man she'd ever met. The personality of "a slug." Four years earlier she was in your chair because of pain. You gave her Novocaine, left her in the chair for an extended period of time for another patient demanding your attention. Barbara blamed you for her wait. Her extraction was complicated. The tooth broke, and you broke into a sweat.

The next day a single vase rose arrives and a note signed Dr. Acer & Staff. Barbara Webb wants answers as she demeans and devalues the rose giver: "We'll never be able to drag David Acer back from wherever he is—I hope it is not too comfortable—and find out the truth."

The mourning Bergalis family
created public service announcements
stating that getting AIDS
can sometimes be as simple
as "pulling a tooth."

The infected patients lined up
to point a finger
to give a just cause
to not be blamed themselves.
You were dead, couldn't refute,
couldn't countersue.

Kimberly, the avowed virgin,
later gave video testimony she had had oral sex, refuting her earlier testimony.
What other things had she lied about?

There have been no other
documented cases of
dentist-to-patient transmission.

The farming town of Nokomis, Illinois,
had a town square
and annual homecoming
celebration with baked pies and decorated floats.
A town of 2,700, with one dentist,
a member of St. Louis Catholic Church, married to a nurse,
a kind man who was hospitalized
in August, 1991. Rumors
swirled, and a sign was
posted on his office door,
Dr. Darr is a victim of AIDS.

After Darr died, his wife remained
silent, until state representative Karen Hasara
told of plans to go public,
to push her agenda for mandatory testing.
Then a reporter published the news.
The townspeople panicked, suggested quarantining.
The health department swooped in,
offered free tests, did 800 in all.

You died a year earlier in Florida,
remained as silent as Darr's wife Donna.
Though there were rumors,
there was never a sign on your door
that the police would have
to be called to remove.

The grandmother had
bowel surgery in the early ’80s,
had a blood transfusion, had
a history of hepatitis,
lymphadenopathy, and herpes—
autoimmune conditions.
All complications of HIV.
These occurred before she saw you.
Before you put on gloves,
asked her to open, injected Novocaine, told
her to floss and use fluoride toothpaste.
This grandmother sued,
blamed you, and
won the settlement.

Sherry Johnson, at age eighteen,
accused David of infecting her.
Her dental procedure, a noninvasive cleaning.
Blamed him on *Larry King Live*, *Good Morning America*,
and in court with Robert Montgomery representing her.
Sherry's mother said David had
"chosen a lifestyle that put him
at risk, but he didn't give my daughter that choice."
Sherry made her own choices. At her diagnosis,
she'd already had six sex partners.
Five of them tested negative.
The sixth couldn't be found.

David's legal documents
state "a single man."
As he signed a letter to go
public, to let his patients know,
there was another confirmed bachelor,
retired in Key West, who had seduced a married
Barbara Webb two decades earlier.

Businesses wanting business
paid for fliers in the Welcome Wagon
envelope. One arrived in Lisa Shoemaker's mailbox.
There was a magnet advertising
the Painless Dentist who gave a
free cleaning for the first visit. She called.
Had several procedures. One
painful, face swelled, and there was
another one where the dentist had coffee breath,
a sore on his neck, and looked sick.
She thought nothing of these things.

She sued after Kimberly and Barbara, when there was
really nothing left, and the media tore
her apart. Labeled Lisa a "carny" and a "slut."
Unlike Kimberly, Lisa hadn't
lied about her past. Didn't
serve up the virgin archetype.

In that time of unknowns and uncertainty,
this is sure. The magnet was
false advertising. Her visits
to Dr. Acer had brought her
great pain and suffering.
Lisa believes in the Lord,
prays and praises him daily,
works on forgiveness for all of the pain
that has been inflicted on her.

James Sharpe worked at
a convenience store in Boston,
made claims similar to Kimberly's,
his HIV due to his own dentist.
Blamed improper cleaning of tools,
1996, and even now
Black men aren't given
the same consideration as white women,
especially an avowed virgin.

Sharpe, unlike Kimberly, had
his sexual life on the stand.
An ex-girlfriend talked of
others, many others.
The jury, maybe savvy from
the Bergalis case, or maybe
less sympathetically swayed due
to the color of his skin,
awarded him nothing.

The inklings of an idea can lead
to something big, can lead to the
deaths of thousands, birth defects,
contamination of water and vegetables.
The Manhattan Project bomb
was created in a Los Alamos lab.
Years later in that same New Mexico lab
something else would be created:
HIV DNA matching test results.

The UK has abandoned using
the DNA matching test
used to align your virus
with that of your patients.

HIV DNA strains should be the same
from the infected mother who
passed it onto her child.
Yet the HIV DNA blood that made
the baby does not match the mother.
The test, like all of the infected
patients' stories, has holes.

There are the odds.
There are the exceptions.
There is the probability.
There is a ratio.
There is everything but a miracle.

Their identifiers covered the alphabet from
A to G, each with their
own story, their own history,
their own incentive. What if
not all of them were swayed
by financial gain?
Maybe scapegoating.
David was easy, the harder things were easier
to forget: the night one blacked out from drinking,
the one-night stand, the shared needle.

The reporters grabbed any quote they could get to create a case that held no logic. John Yecs said David Acer "was awful slow" during a root canal. As if a patient ever thought a root canal went quickly. Another called the dentist "unconscionably sloppy." David researched with health-care officials, changed sterilizing procedures, and wrote a letter to his past patients while dying. Another journalist twisted a hygienist's quote about how Acer said he had ulcers and then resolved to not "get upset about anything." As if that said something bad about his character.

On October 18, 1995, the *Palm Beach Post*,
consumed over morning coffee,
left on the table of break rooms,
carried the first headline:
"Fort Pierce Woman Contracted Aids From Her Dentist."
This is how the story was served,
without the legalized buffering language
of "claimed" or "alleged."

The CDC report comparing your blood
to the defendants'
stated noncommittally,
high degree of similarity of strains
strongly suggest that
transmission
might have occurred.

These are the words the
lawyer Robert Montgomery used:
solid proof of transmission
irrefutable evidence of causation.

The day after your letter was published,
stating your innocence,
Montgomery held a press conference:
Kimberly as the centerpiece,
her virginity, the perfect victim,
to rewrite your final letter as a lie.

David Horowitz wrote a book comparing David to serial killers and in it mused that his own life might be in danger for his disclosures. Horowitz also created a relaxation tape for those who feared going to the dentist. Everybody was interested in profit. Television ads showed a woman entering her dentist's office with her own pouch of tools for him to use. You could buy them too, by simply calling the number on the screen.

Never thought to be at high-risk for infection, Kimberly blamed her dentist. The last year of her life, she lobbied for health-care workers to get mandatorily tested. Her lawyer and parents cheer-leading at her side. Kimberly claimed she wanted HIV workers to disclose, not lose their jobs. Said how harmful positive health-care workers were. On the same *48 Hours* she was featured on, a gay HIV-positive man looked for a dentist, went into office after office for dental care, and was denied treatment.

David wrote, "It is my desire to die in private peace and quiet with as much dignity as possible."

Kimberly wrote, "If laws are not formed to provide protection, then my suffering and death was in vain."

Neither received what they wanted.

Kimberly visited a new dentist,
the paper bib was clipped around her neck,
Kimberly leaned back in the
dental chair, before your death and
after your retirement, and said nothing
of her HIV status. She didn't disclose
the very thing she later wanted,
demanded of health-care workers.
Debra, a hygienist who worked with you,
cleaned her teeth, remembered her
from the old office, didn't know about
the virus in her patient's blood
or how her accusations would go viral.

I imagine two men
parked on the Tamiami Trail
walking into the cemetery
at dusk, kicking the grave markers,
looking for a loose one
or to jostle one loose. They find one
near the sundial—
the marker for David Johnson Acer.
They hold onto it as they search
for others. They're not interested in your life,
early death at forty-one, the reasons behind it,
your long suffering in silence before
physical suffering and pain, the lesions
that covered your body. They are interested
in money, what this marker of
your life, melted down, could get.

After Sondra Bergalis's death
her father blamed the bars
for Sondra's binge drinking.
He said their cheap drinks were too
enticing for the young.
He was a protective father
not seeing his daughters'—
the middle Kimberly,
the youngest Sondra—
responsibility, fallibility.

Wearing two paper wristbands from bars
and no seatbelt, Sondra drove
a Honda Prelude, registered
under her father's name,
down the wrong side of the highway.

At age sixty-eight, Victor A. Acer moved to
Florida to help care for his stepson
dying of a disease little was known
about. Later living in the house
he and Harriet inherited.
Nothing left in his dead son's estate.
Hospitals, courts, and past clients drained it all.
Even a year after David's death, the answering
machine tape recorded voices of hate.
The mailbox consumed with
correspondence about David's deserved death,
burning in hell, of him being a murderer.
Victor helped Harriet clean the house
of clippings and notes made
by David on how to not transmit the virus.

Victor, age seventy-three, on March 27, 1995,
walked into the backyard
past the pool David installed,
hidden behind the privacy
fence David built,
put a gun in his mouth
and pulled the trigger.

Harriet Acer said goodnight to husband Victor at 10 p.m. Five years had passed since her son David died, yet the news about him hadn't died down. She woke up after midnight, and Victor wasn't in bed. She walked around and couldn't find him. Called 911. The police found him dead on the back lawn. A .25 caliber wound on the roof of his mouth. The gun near his body was usually kept in his file drawer. There was no note. She told the police he had talked about suicide but had been "depressed over financial problems."

He stood six feet tall
wrestled on the high school team,
played tennis and racquetball
with friends, flew planes over the Gulf of
Mexico, completed the rigors of dental school.
His ambition was palpable, ever present.
He was driven and alone,
desperate at times, and lonely,
wanting love, and then AIDS
happened. Everything he built
he was going to lose.
He had been saving up for
the future and realized
that he might not have one.

In the Palm Beach Hospice
there was constant diarrhea,
the thick white yeast of thrush
coating his mouth and throat.
On continuous oxygen, Kaposi
sores on his legs, chest, and in his
lungs. A catheter inserted
into his urethra. He had told
his stepfather Victor
he hoped for a cure. That hope
died with him or just moments before.

The lights from the casino machines
blinked and brightened,
begged for attention.
I sat in the corner at one of the slot machines
and inserted my card to play.
It was the corner of the arcade
where David Acer's office once was.
I wanted to stand on that floor, see
the windows patients looked out on when
in David's chair. On the last day
of my last trip to the Treasure Coast,
I stood in the building where all of it
happened. This was where history
was made and rewritten and misinterpreted
and misdirected. The machine
had a button instead of a side lever.
I played Robin Hood.
Electronic reels of three images that need
to be aligned to win.
On the ground that I stood, I was
taking risks. The patients took risks, unknowingly.
David took risks, unknowingly.
There are no sure things.
No one comes out clean.
Everyone feels cheated.

SELECTED BIBLIOGRAPHY

"AIDS Ad Features Bergalis." *Fort Pierce Tribune*, November 6, 1993.

AIDS: CDC's Investigation of HIV Transmissions by a Dentist: Report to the Chairman, Human Resources and Intergovernmental Relations Subcommittee, Committee on Government Operations, House of Representatives. Washington, DC: US General Accounting Office, 1992.

Almond, Steven. "Critical Condition: AIDS Researcher of High Repute. Proprietor of a Glamorous Miami Beach Spa. Target of a Federal Criminal Probe. The Many Sides of Dr. Lionel Resnick." *Miami New Times*, March 9, 1995.

Altman, Lawrence K. "AIDS and a Dentist's Secrets." *New York Times*, June 6, 1993.

———. "The Doctor's World: AIDS Mystery That Won't Go Away: Did Dentist Infect 6 Patients?" *New York Times*, July 5, 1994.

Barr, Stephen, "The 1990 Florida Dental Investigation: Is the Case Really Closed?" *Annals of Internal Medicine* 124, no. 2 (1996): 250–54.

———. "What if the Dentist Didn't Do It?" *New York Times*, April 16, 1994.

Barton, Eric Alan. "Bullet Bob." *Broward–Palm Beach New Times* (Fort Lauderdale, FL), April 28, 2005.

Bell, Maya. "Doctor Disputes Dentist Infected Patients with AIDS." *Orlando Sentinel*, May 18, 1994.

Breo, Dennis. "The Dental AIDS Cases—Murder or an Unsolvable Mystery?" *Journal of the American Medical Association* 270 (1993): 2732–34.

———. "Meet Kimberly Bergalis—The Patient in the 'Dental AIDS Case.'" *Journal of the American Medical Association* 264 no. 15 (1990): 2018–19.

———. "Unreported Findings Shed New Light on HIV Dental Case." *AIDS Alert*, July 1, 1991, 121.

———. "What Kind of Dentist Was David Acer?" *AIDS Alert*, June 1991, 133–37.

Bridgwater, Mark "Bergalis' Dad Pushes Ad Blitz: 'Remember My Words' Media Campaign Unveiled." *Palm Beach Post*, October 27, 1992.

Brown, David. "The 1990 Florida Dental Investigation: Theory and Fact." *Annals of Internal Medicine* 124 no. 2 (1996): 255–56.

Burkett, Elinor. *The Gravest Show on Earth: America in the Age of AIDS.* Boston: Houghton Mifflin, 1995.

Centers for Disease Control. "Epidemiologic Notes and Reports Update: Transmission of HIV Infection during Invasive Dental Procedures—Florida." *Morbidity and Mortality Weekly Report* (MMWR) (Centers for Disease Control and Prevention), June 14, 1991, 377–81. www.cdc.gov/mmwr/preview/mmwrhtml/00014428.htm.

———. "Investigations of Persons Treated by HIV-Infected Health-Care Workers—United States." *Morbidity and Mortality Weekly Report* (MMWR) (Centers for Disease Control and Prevention), May 7, 1993, 329–31, 337. www.cdc.gov/mmwr/preview/mmwrhtml/00020479.htm.

———. "Possible Transmission of Human Immunodeficiency Virus to a Patient during an Invasive Dental Procedure." *Morbidity and Mortality Weekly Report* (MMWR) (Centers for Disease Control and Prevention), July 27, 1990, 489–93. www.cdc.gov/mmwr/preview/mmwrhtml/00001679.htm.

Certificate of Death: Acer, Victor. Filed 26 Mar 1995. State of Florida, State of Florida Office of the Medical Examiner. File No. ME-95-19-200.

Crandall, Keith A. "Intraspecific Phylogenetics: Support for Dental Transmission of Human Immunodeficiency Virus." *Journal of Virology* 69, no. 4 (1995): 2351–56.

"Dentist's Legacy of AIDS Still Lives On." Cox News Service, December 21, 1992.

Dorschner John. "The Doctor Will Infect You Now." *Tropic: The Miami Herald Sunday Magazine*, October 27, 1991, 7–11, 16.

Drake, Donald C., "How Patients Got AIDS from Dentist Unresolved." Knight Ridder Services, June 22, 1991.

Duesberg, Peter. *Inventing the AIDS Virus*. Washington, DC: Regnery Publishing, 1995.

Evans, Dan. "Ranch Dedicates Garden to Bergalis." *San Luis Obispo Tribune*, January 27, 1992.

"Evidence in Acer Case Questioned." *Fort Pierce Tribune,* February 25, 1993.

Folstad, Kim. "Patient 'E: Life after David Acer.'" *Palm Beach Post,* September 3, 2000.

Gallagher, Joh. "AIDS Media Circus: Hype and Hysteria behind the Headlines." *Advocate*, Aug 10, 1991, 32.

Gentile, Ben. "Doctors and AIDS." *Newsweek*, July 7, 1991, 48.

Hammett, Yvette C., Michael Colt, and Michael Cheek. "Kimberly Bergalis Dies, AIDS: Bergalis, Fort Pierce Woman Brought the AIDS Fight to Broader Audience." *Stuart (FL) News*, December 9, 1991.

Henry, William A., III. "Patient A: Asking Who Is Innocent." *Time*, May 17, 1993.

Hiaasen, Rob. "Dr. Acer's Deadly Secret: How AIDS Joined the Lives of a Dentist and His Patients." *Palm Beach Post*, September 29, 1991.

———. "The Sad Story of 'Patient G.'" *Palm Beach Post*, July 12, 1993.

Hillis David M. "Application and Accuracy of Molecular Phylogenies." *Science*, April 29, 1994, 671.

Hogan, Katie, and Nancy L. Roth. *Gendered Epidemic: Representations of Women in the Age of AIDS*. New York: Routledge, 1998.

Hood, Carra Leah. "Reading the News: Activism, Authority, Audience." PhD thesis, Yale University.

Horowitz, Leonard. *Deadly Innocence: The Kimberly Bergalis Case.* Rockport, MA: Tetrahedron, 1994.

———. *Emerging Viruses: AIDS and Ebola: Nature, Accident or Intentional*. Rockport, MA: Tetrahedron, 1995.

Houck, Jeff. "Auction Raises Spirits of Sixth Acer Victim." *Palm Beach Post*, August 18, 1993.

Hughes, John. "Positive." *Sun Sentinel* (Fort Lauderdale, FL), September 26, 1990.

Jackson, Stephanie L. "Bergalis Leaves Porsche to Aunt: $60,000 Willed to AIDS Group, Research." *Palm Beach Post*, January 14, 1992.

———. "Hundreds Mourn Bergalis: Fort Pierce Woman Was 'Voice of All AIDS sufferers.'" *Palm Beach Post*, December 10, 1991.

Johnson, Bonnie. "The Dentist and the Patients: An AIDS Mystery." *People*, October 22, 1990, 70.

Jones, Colman. "AIDS: Words from the Front." *Spin*, August 1994, 79.

Lambert, Bruce. "Kimberly Bergalis Is Dead at 23: Symbol of Debate over AIDS Tests." *New York Times*, December 9, 1991.

Lane, Teresa. "Bergalis Details Sexual Past to Support AIDS Lawsuit." *Palm Beach Post*, January 8, 1991.

Large, Maggie. "Bergalis' Sister Killed in Car Crash: Sondra Bergalis Was the Youngest Sister of Kimberly Bergalis, Who Contracted HIV from Her Dentist and Died of AIDS in 1991." *Fort Pierce Tribune*, November 18, 2000.

Lasalandra, Michael. "AIDS Kills Bergalis' Lawyer's Son." *Palm Beach Post*, January 25, 1995.

———. "Split CDC Had No Choice but to Publish AIDS Case." *Palm Beach Post*, November 14, 1990.

———. "Study Casts Doubt on Bergalis-Acer AIDS Link." *Palm Beach Post*, February 25, 1993.

Lauritsen, John. "The AIDS War: Lies and Censorship in Coverage of the Epidemic. *New York Native*, August 12, 1991. virusmyth.com/aids/hiv/jlwar.htm.

Leen, Clifford. "The Dental AIDS Mystery." *British Medical Journal* 307, no. 6899 (1993): 332+.

Leinwand, Donna, "AIDS Victim Fights Disease, Doubters." Knight-Ridder Newspapers, November 14, 1990.

———. "Medical Group Assail CDC Dentist-AIDS Link." *Miami Herald*, November 11, 1990.

Martin, Douglas. "Robert Montgomery, 78, a Big-Case Lawyer, Dies." *New York Times*, August 7, 2008.

McMullan, Dawn. "High Schools Might Study Bergalis Case," *Fort Pierce Tribune,* June 30, 1991

———. "Magnolia Attests to Kimberly's Magnificence." *Fort Pierce Tribune,* June 30, 1991.

———. "Remembering Kim." *Stuart (FL) News*, December 6, 1991.

Midwinter, Janet. "Death-bed Confession of the Girl Who Got AIDS from Dentist Is Dividing America." *Mail on Sunday* (London, UK), June 26, 1994.

Milstone, Erik. "Looking for Trouble: When Big Businesses Hire Private Gumshoes, Things Can Get Sticky." *Palm Beach Post*, December 1, 1991.

Moore, Pat. "Acer's Parents Ordered to Answer Questions: Attorneys for Patient Seek Records." *Palm Beach Post*, October 31, 1991.

———. "Bergalis' Sister Killed in Crash in Tallahassee." *Palm Beach Post*, November 18, 2000.

———. "HIV-Infected Patient Settles Suit against Dentist's Estate." *Palm Beach Post*, October 25, 1995.

———. "Investigator Can't Be Questioned; Judge Rules against Man Suing Acer." *Palm Beach Post*, October 17, 1991.

———. "Prostitutes Hired in Inquiry of Acer Patient, Lawyers Say." *Palm Beach Post*, October 10, 1991.

Myers, Gerald. "Molecular Investigation of HIV Transmission." *Annals of Internal Medicine* 121, no. 11 (1994): 889–90.

Nesmith, Susannah A. "Latest Acer Victim a Reluctant Crusader." *Palm Beach Post*, August 9, 1993.

"Ohioan Is 3d Dental Patient to Die from AIDS Infection." *New York Times*, July 8, 1993.

Ostrom, Neenyah. "The Age of Chronic Immune Dysfunction." *New York Native*, July 25, 1994.

———. "Sex, Lies and Videotape: CDC Finding in 'AIDS' Dentist Case Contested; Furor Raised over Access to Data." *New York Native*, February 17, 1992.

Palca, Joseph. "The Case of the Florida Dentist." *Science*, January 24, 1992, 392–94.

———. "CDC Closes the Case of the Florida Dentist." *Science* 256, May 22, 1992, 1130–31.

Pallesen, Tim. "Doctor: Acer Didn't Infect His Patients." *Palm Beach Post*, June 20, 1994.

Plummer, William. "Dr. Acer's Sixth Victim: Sherry Johnson, 18, Learns She Too Apparently Got HIV from Her Dentist." *People*, May 24, 1993. https://people.com/archive/dr-acers-sixth-victim-vol-39-no-20.

Rial, Martha. "Other Patients Infected by Dr. David Acer." *Fort Pierce Tribune,* December 6, 1992.

Ritter, Malcom. "Gene Evidence Questioned in Patients' AIDS Infections." Associated Press, February 25, 1993.

Rom, Mark C. *Fatal Extraction: The Story behind the Florida Dentist Accused of Infecting His Patients with HIV and Poisoning Public Health*. San Francisco: Jossey-Bass, 1997.

Runnells, Robert R. *AIDS in the Dental Office? The Story of Kimberly Bergalis and Dr. David Acer*. Fruit Heights, UT: I.C. Publications, 1993.

Ryan, Laura, "Kimberly's Legacy." *Fort Pierce Tribune,* December 6, 1992.

Saitz, Greg. "Lawyer Tackled Tough Case—and Won." *Fort Pierce Tribune,* September 8, 1992.

———. "One Patient Overlooked in Acer Case." *Fort Pierce Tribune*, June 15.

———. "Patient G Joins AIDs-Testing Fight." *Fort Pierce Tribune,* August 14, 1991.

Samples Eve. "Mysterious Ad Triggers Memories of Controversial Dentist with AIDS." *Stuart (FL) News*, September 16, 2012.

Santich, Kate. "The Fate of Patient B, Barbara Webb, Who Caught the Aids Virus from the Dentist Who Infected Kimberly Bergalis, Uses Humor and Passion to Teach Others While Searching for a Reason that Might Make Sense of Her Tragedy." *Orlando Sentinel Florida Magazine*, September 27, 1992.

"Sith Case Offers No Clues in Florida HIV Cluster Mystery." *AIDS Alert*, July 1, 1993.

Smith, Cheryl. "Gallery's Display Personalizes Bergalis." *Fort Pierce Tribune,* January 26, 1992.

Smith, Jeff, "Lisa Shoemaker, Known as Patient E, Works to Prevent HIV." *MyNorth.com*, January 21, 2010. https://mynorth.com/2010/01/lisa-shoemaker-known-as-patient-e-works-to-prevent-hiv.

Smith, Temple F. "The Continuing Case of the Florida Dentist." *Science* May 22, 1992, 1155–56 .

Smothers, Ronald. "Teen-Ager with H.I.V. Tells of Anger and Isolation. *New York Times*, May 8, 1993.

Soghanalian, Shirley. "The Mysterious Dr. Acer." *Tropic: The Miami Herald Sunday Magazine*, December 8, 1991, 2.

Stroh, M. "DNA Solves AIDS Epidemiological Whodunit." *Science News*, May 23, 1992, 341.

Tagliarini, Lynda. "Play May Tell Life of Bergalis." *Fort Pierce Tribune,* November 12, 1991.

Trontz, Ian. "Kimberly Bergalis: Five Years after Her Death; 'She Wanted to Protect Other People's Lives.'" *Palm Beach Post*, December 8, 1996.

Wallace, Mike. "Kimberly's Story: Each of the Six People Who Claim They Got AIDS from Dentist Dr. David Acer Were Found to Have Had Other Sources for the Disease." *60 Minutes*, June 19, 1994, transcript.

Webb, Barbara. "Others Will Take Up Kimberly Bergalis' Struggle." *Stuart (FL) News*, December 9, 1991.

Weiss, Stanley H., and Judith D. Leschek. "HIV Era Occupational Exposures and Risks." In *AIDS and Other Manifestations of HIV Infection*, 4th ed., edited by Gary P. Wormser, 811–38. Amsterdam, Netherlands: Elsevier Science, 2004.

ACKNOWLEDGMENTS

I'M GRATEFUL FOR the early readers of this manuscript, who gave their time, input, edits, and energy into helping me shape this material: Collin Kelley, Darin Klein, Tim Miller, and David Trinidad. Before it was a manuscript, Terry Wolverton and Amy Gerstler gave great guidance on a handful of poems.

Thanks to those who hosted and housed me at times while I researched in Florida and wrote in cities across the country: Peter Nguyen and Grant Kalinowski, Irvin Lin and AJ Bates, Stephanie Recht and Ed Rook, Tyler Schnoebelen, Natalie Goldberg, Rob Wilder, Brian Rush, the Cramer Family, the Roberts-Watson family, Christopher Honey and Riley West, and Thaddeus Root and Desmond Clark.

I appreciate those who called when I placed the newspaper ad asking about David and those I called directly. Your information, years later, was invaluable in helping me to tell the full story.

Thanks to Jim Harper, Steve Pride, and Brian DeShazor for advice on interviewing. Bryan Cooper and Halle Mares for permission rights. To my writer friends, who gave great modeling and encouraging words: Bernard Cooper, David Francis, James Gavin, Kim Dower, Ian MacKinnon, and Clement Goldberg.

To my friends who gave support as I talked through challenges and issues with this material: David K. Johnson, Kimberly Dupuis,

Layla Ross, Brett Freedman, Jenny Waters, Jill Stansbury, Juliette Aiyana, Patricia Walters, Gabriel Blanco, and Heidi Arnott.

To those friends who have aided my life and career in innumerable ways: BJ Millan, Michael S. Kelley, Carol Lena, Lisa Kereszi, Karina Wilson, Karen Malbon, Amber Slater-Raymond, David Roman, Jasper Sage, Martha Roper, Hunter Lee Hughes, Shannon Headley, Shirley E. Taylor, Andy Cordero, Nancy Comeau, Tod Macofsky, Michael Saul, David Stumpff and Don Tinling, Sanford Thompson, and Alex Bazley.

There are those who helped me bring *A Quilt for David* across the finish line: Jonny McGovern, Evans Vestal Ward, John Morgan Wilson, Pietro Gamino, Jim Gladstone, David Leonardo Padilla, and Mattilda Bernstein Sycamore.

I want to recognize some of the archives and institutions that made research possible: ONE Archives, Stonewall Library, Tom of Finland Foundation, June Mazer Lesbian Archives, UCLA Library, Hoover High School, Ohio State University Library, Martin Country Courthouse, Lisa Shoemaker for generously sharing her archives, Los Angeles County Library, and Beyond Baroque.

Endless gratitude for my dear friend, agent, and skillful editor Amy Scholder, who believed deeply in me and the aim of this book. Thank you, Stacey Lewis, who guided this book out into the world; Gerilyn Attebery for the beautiful design; and Elaine Katzenberger for saying yes and including me in the City Lights family of writers. I'm beyond thrilled and grateful.

PHOTO BY GABRIEL GOLDBERG

ABOUT THE AUTHOR

STEVEN REIGNS, Los Angeles poet and educator, was appointed the first Poet Laureate of West Hollywood. He has two previous collections, *Inheritance* and *Your Dead Body Is My Welcome Mat*, and over a dozen chapbooks. Reigns edited *My Life Is Poetry*, showcasing his students' work from the first-ever autobiographical poetry workshop for LGBTQIA+ seniors. Reigns has lectured and taught writing workshops around the country to LGBTQIA+ youth and people living with HIV. He worked for a decade as an HIV test counselor in Florida and Los Angeles. Currently he is touring *The Gay Rub*, an exhibition of rubbings from LGBTQIA+ landmarks around the world, and has a private practice as a psychotherapist.

StevenReigns.com \\ TheGayRub.com

DAVID JOHNSON

ACER

NOV. 11, 1949

SEPT. 3, 1990